THE HANDMADE ALPHABET

Laura Rankin

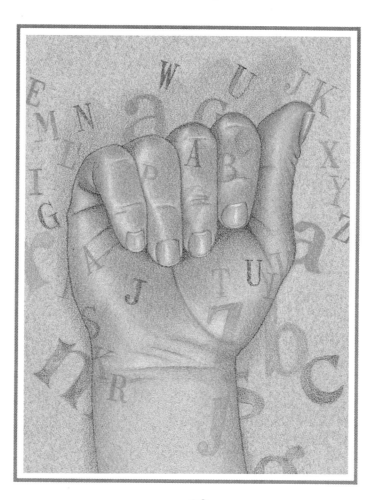

DIAL BOOKS NEW YORK

For Nick and Brendan, with love

The artist and publisher appreciate the help of
Alan R. Barwiolek, M.A.,
American Sign Language/Deaf Culture Consultant.

Published by Dial Books
A Division of Penguin Books USA Inc.
375 Hudson Street
New York, New York 10014

3 5 7 9 10 8 6 4

Library of Congress Cataloging in Publication Data
Rankin, Laura.
The handmade alphabet / by Laura Rankin.
p.   cm.
Summary: Presents the manual alphabet,
used in American Sign Language.
ISBN 0-8037-0974-9 (trade). — ISBN 0-8037-0975-7 (library)
1. Deaf — Means of communication. [1. Alphabet. 2. Deaf.]
I. Title.
HV2480.R36 1991   419 — dc20   [E]   90-24593   CIP   AC

The art for each picture consists of colored pencil on charcoal paper,
which is scanner-separated and reproduced in full color.

Artist's Note

My older stepson is deaf. For the first eighteen years of his life he moved with dignity yet difficulty through the hearing world, relying primarily on the complex art of lipreading for his verbal understanding. Then he went to Gallaudet University in Washington, D.C., and learned American Sign Language. As a visual language it was completely accessible to him and allowed him to share ideas fully. Through it he gained more thorough understanding and total communication.

The manual alphabet, an integral part of American Sign Language, was my first contact with signing. As an outsider to deaf culture, my abilities in this mode are limited. However, my respect is deep and it is my wish that this introduction to the alphabet begin to open the world of sign communication to all who see this book.

—LAURA RANKIN
Buffalo, New York

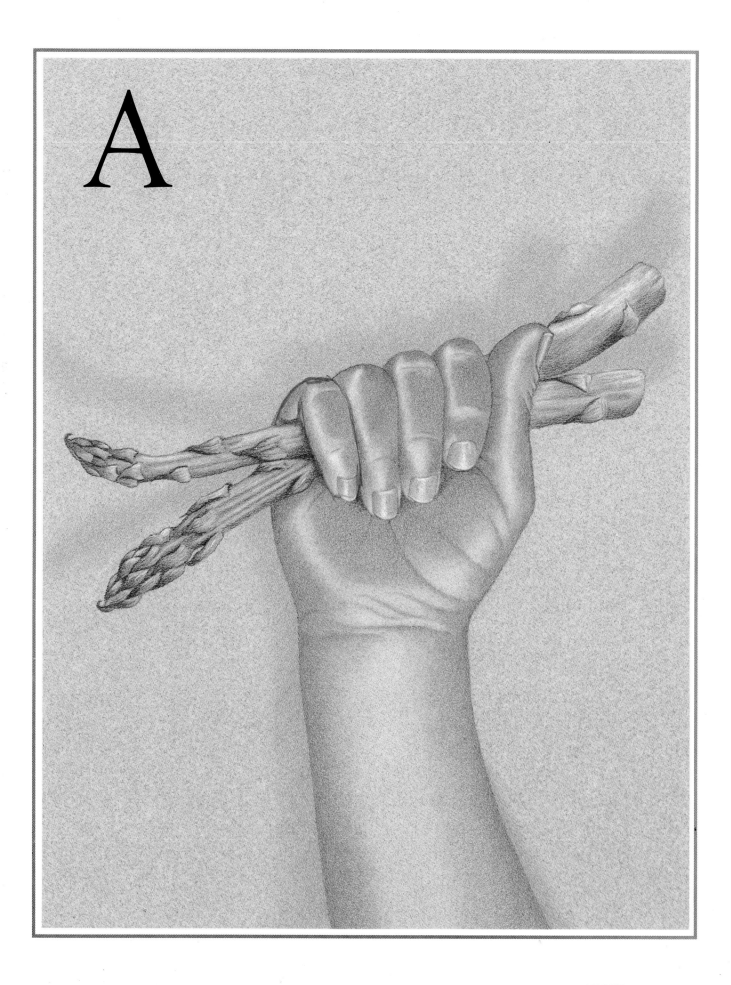

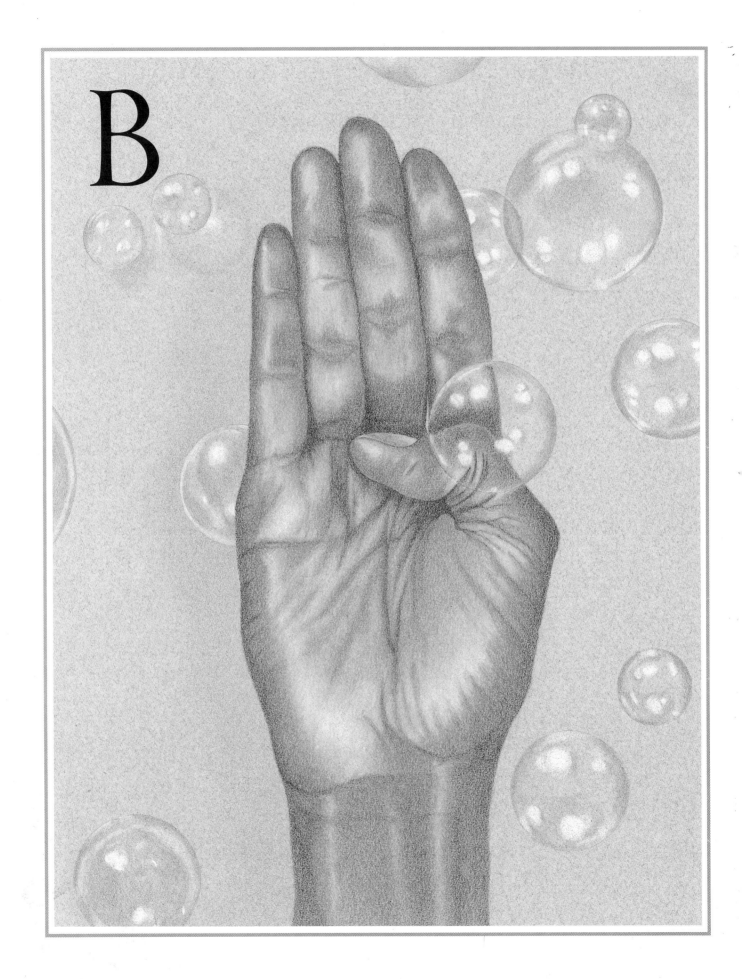

D

E

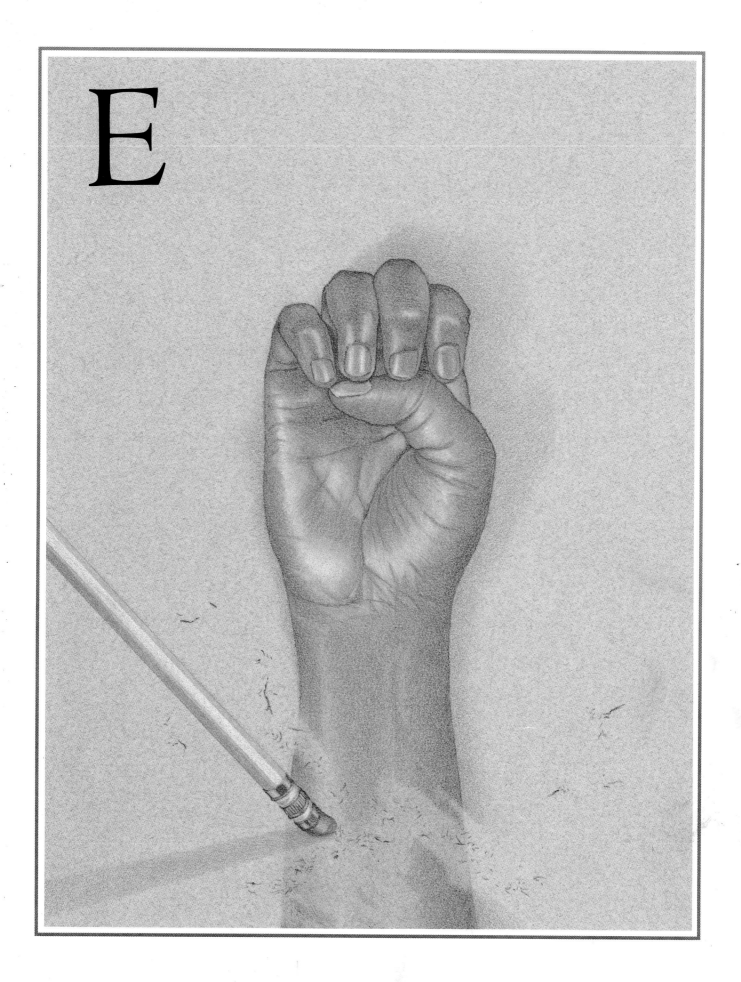

G

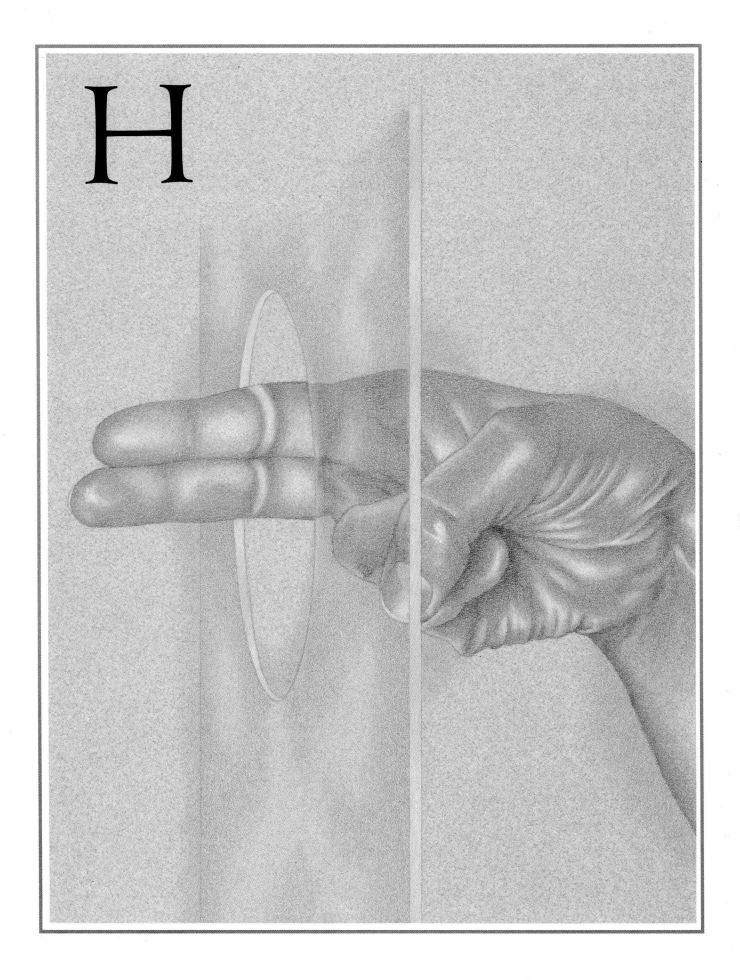

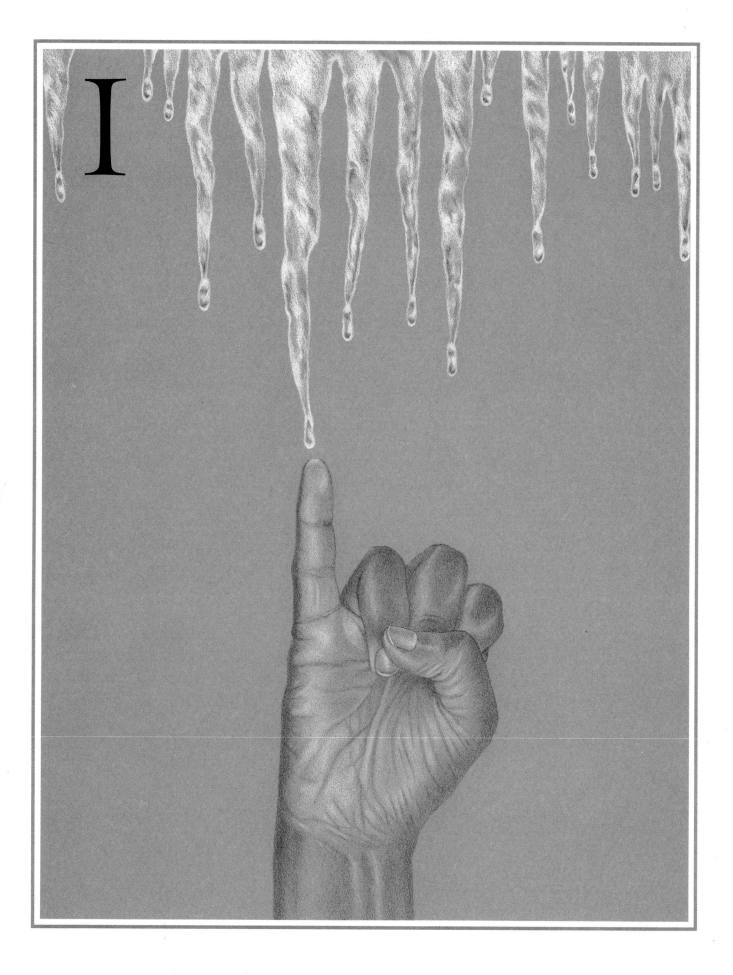

K

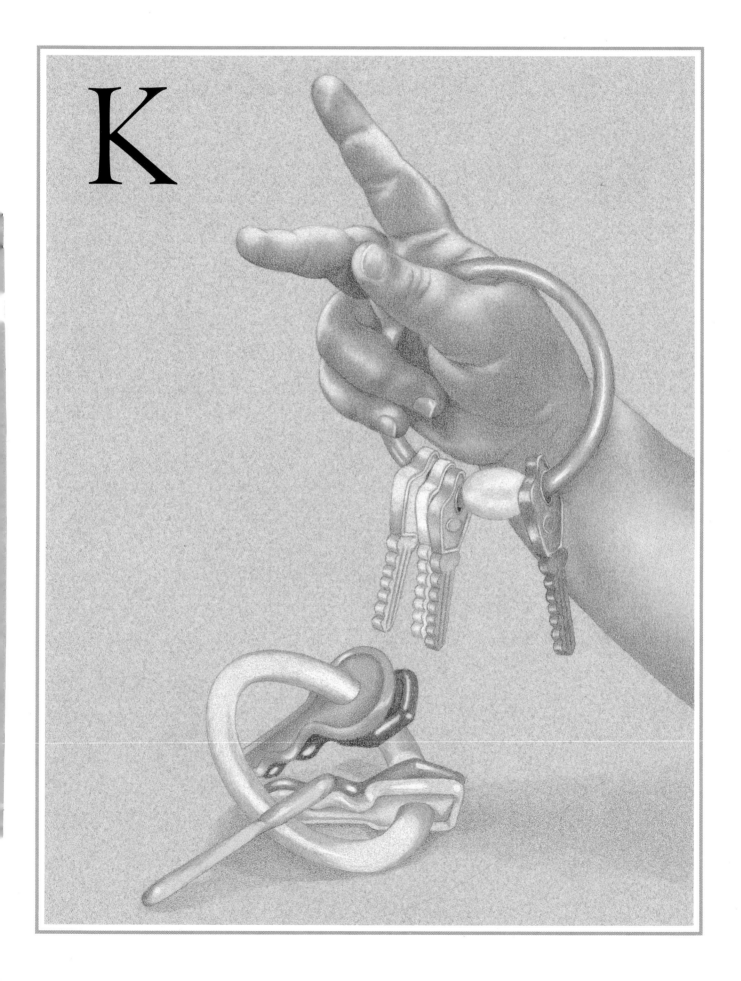

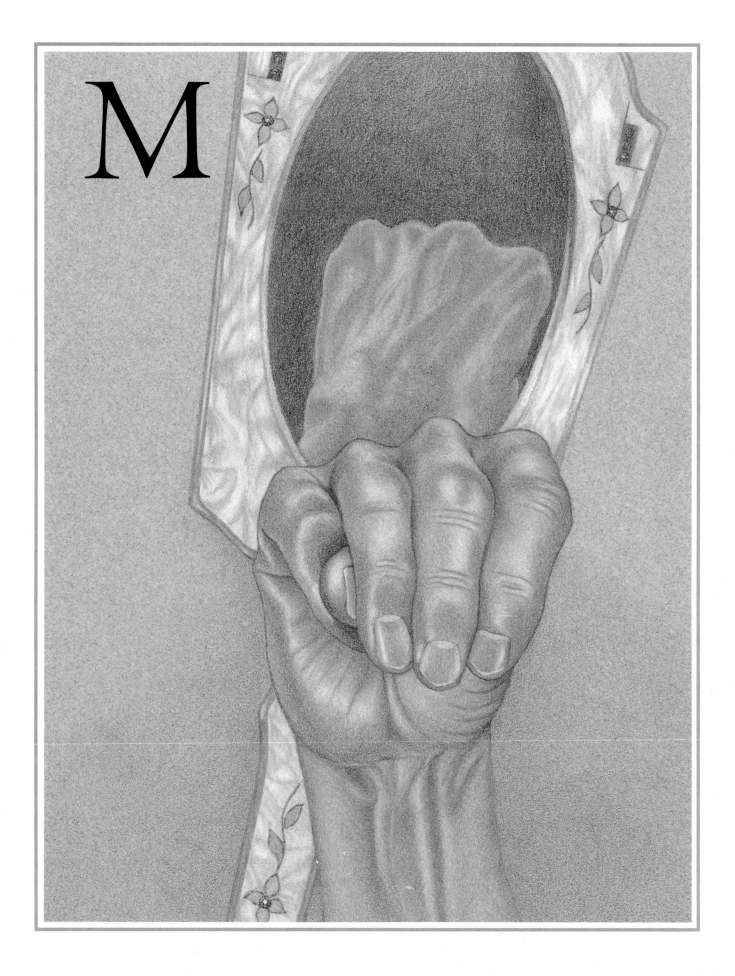

N

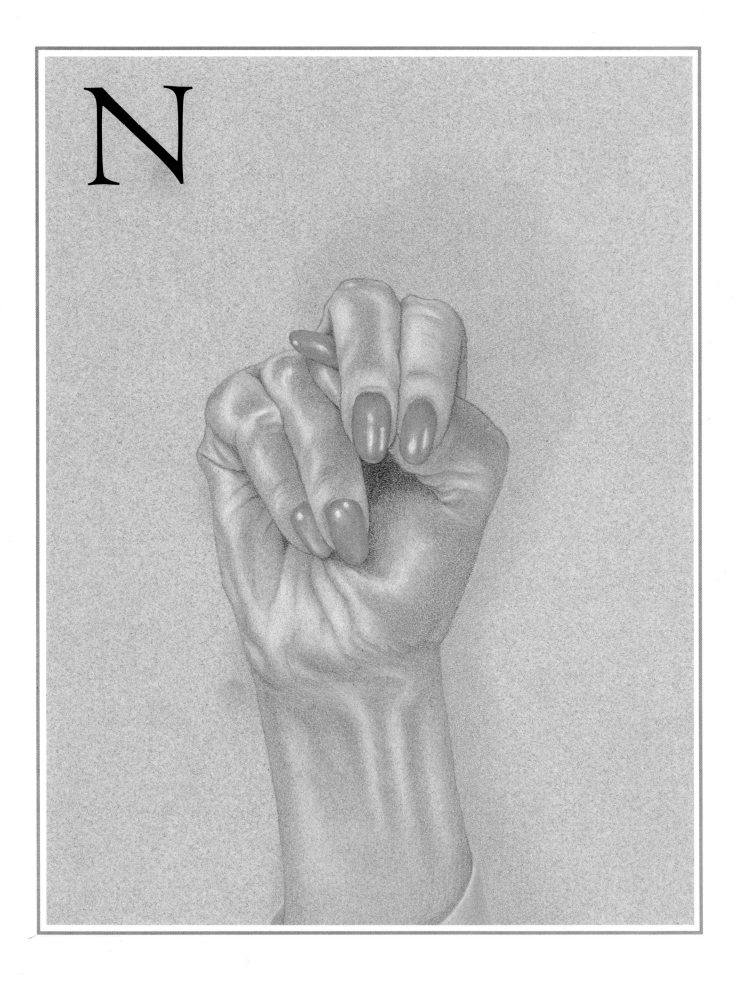

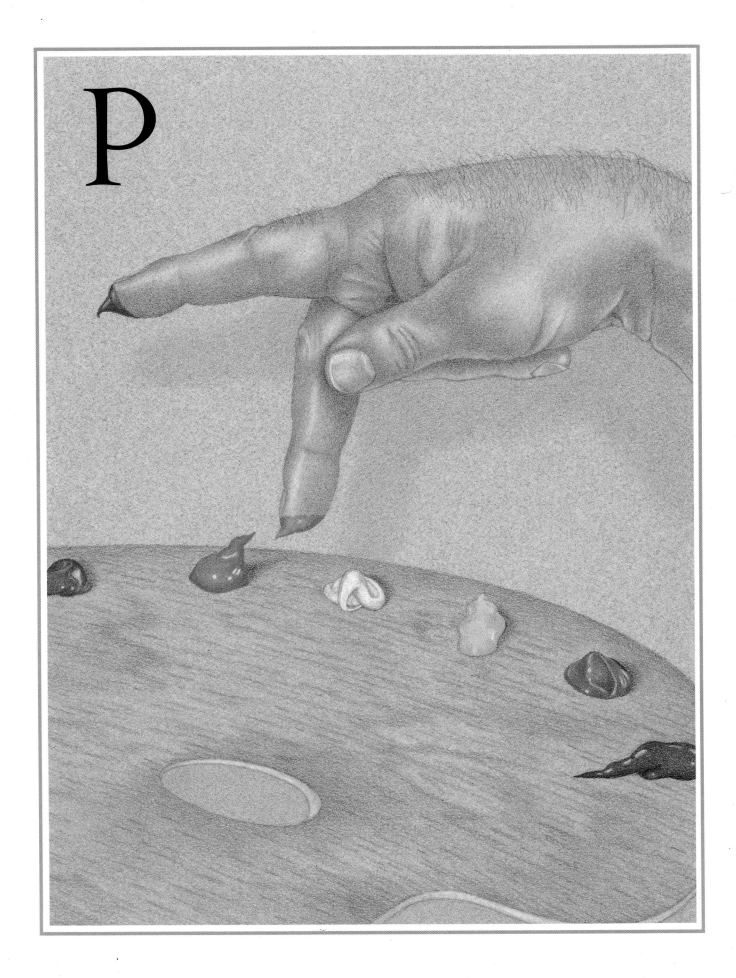

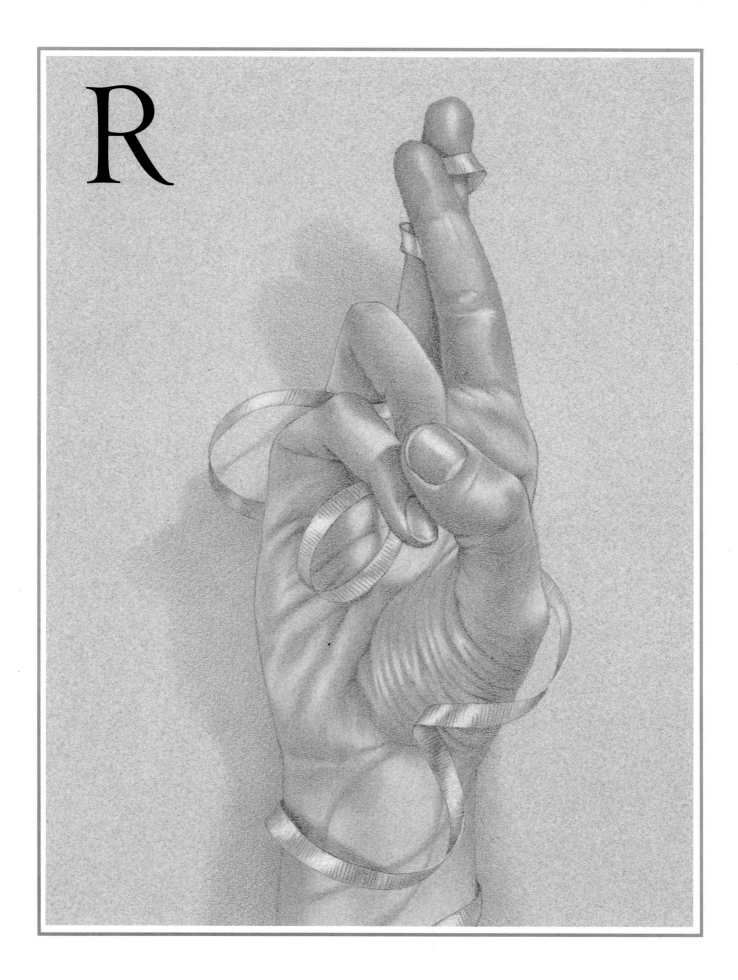

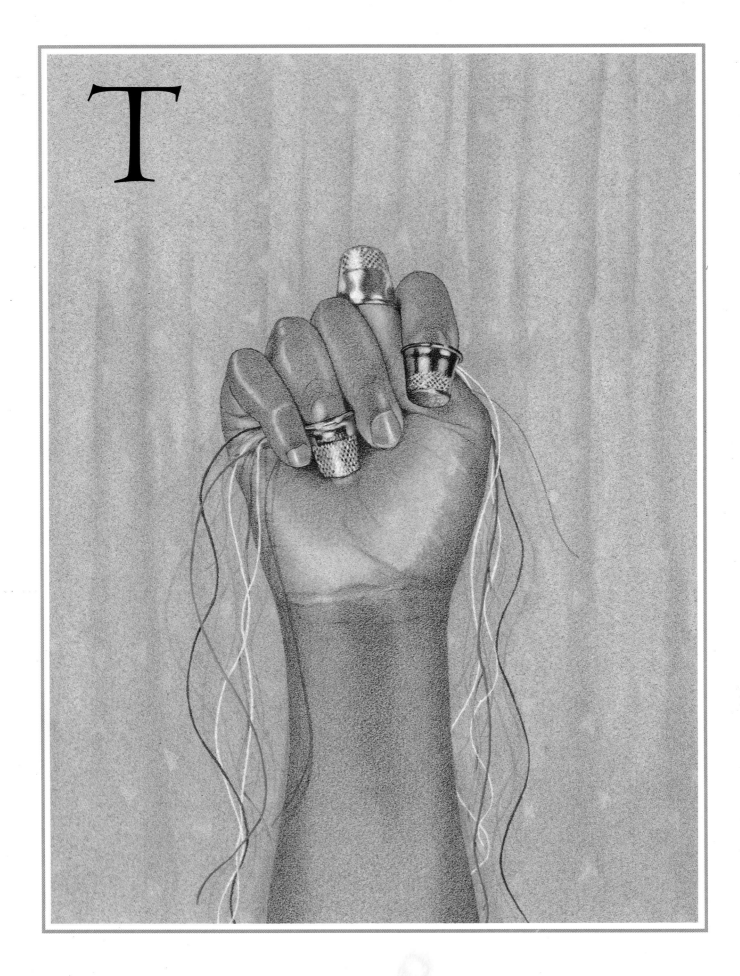

V

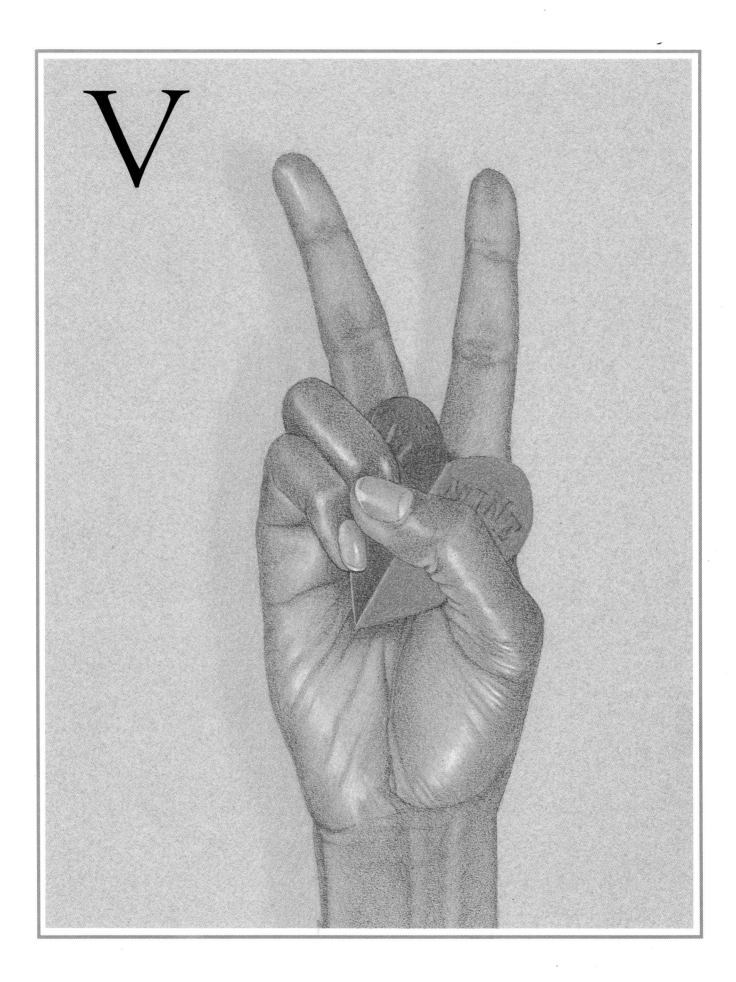

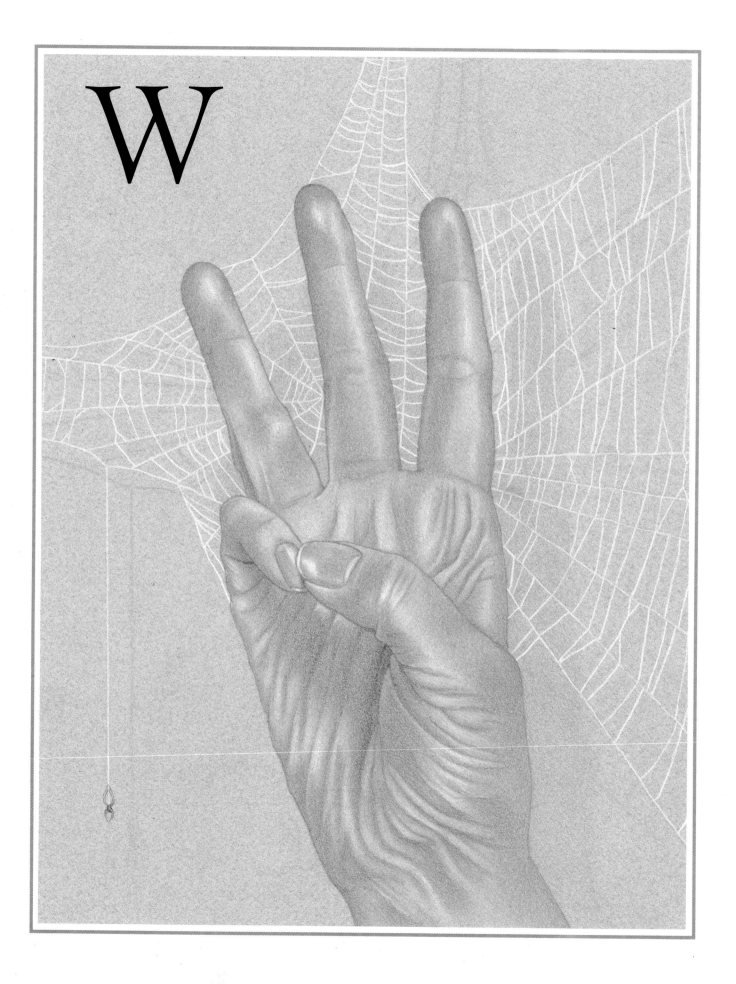

X

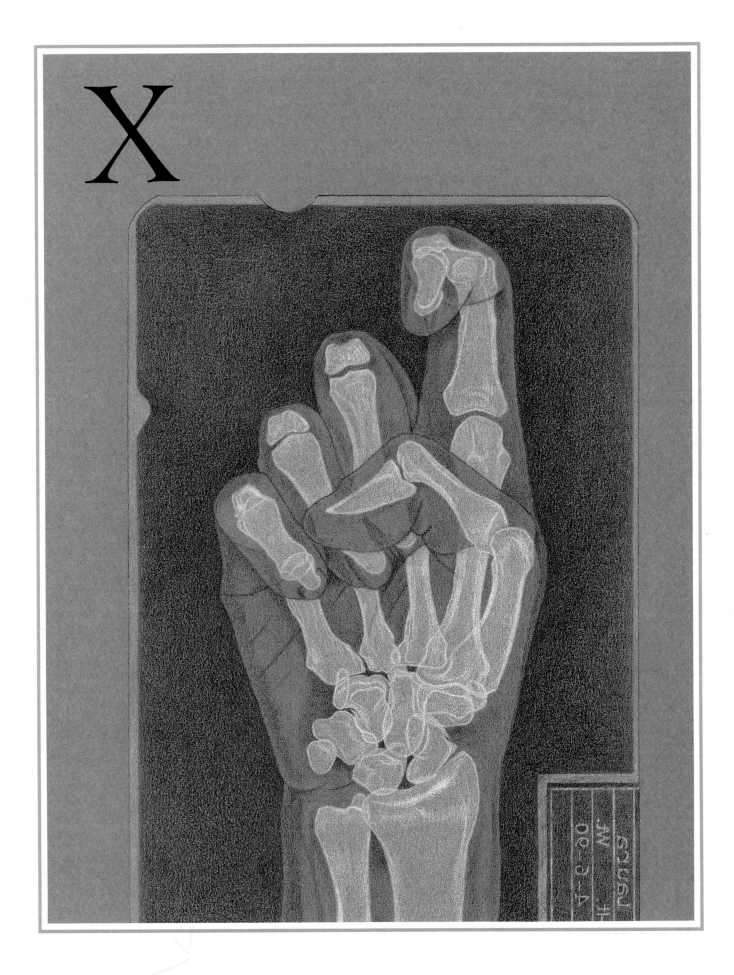

Y

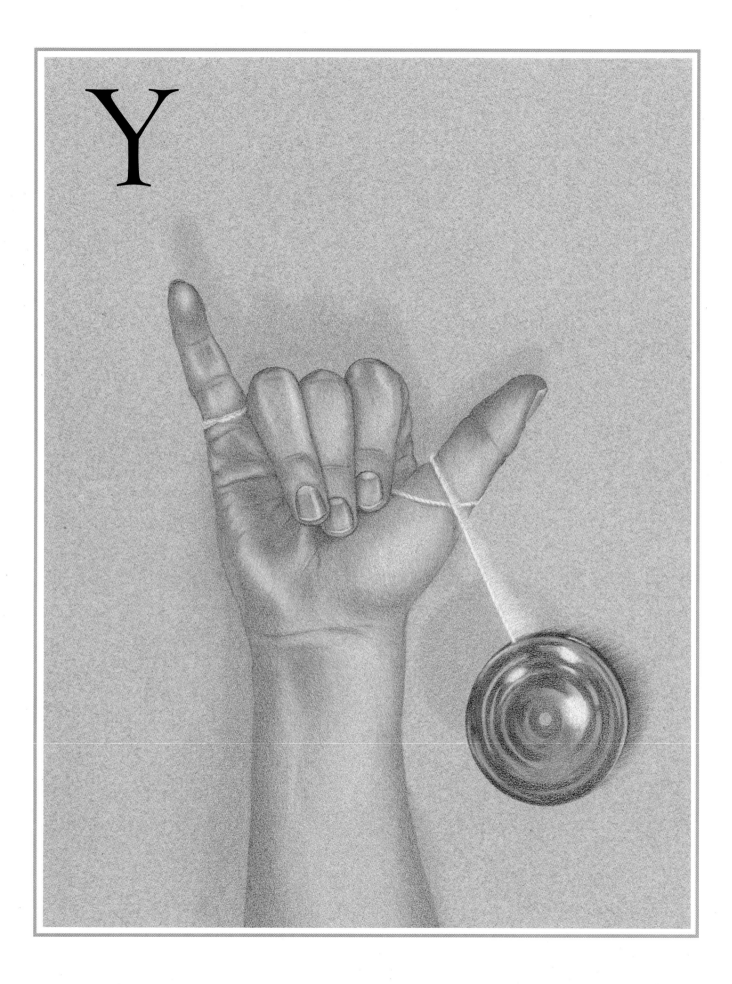

Z

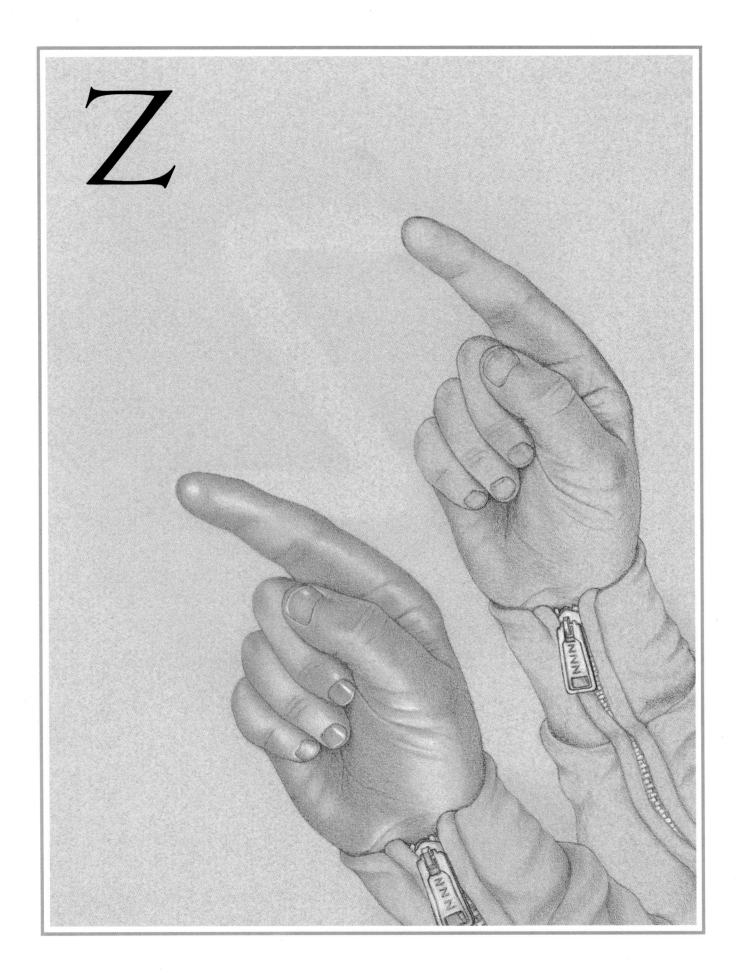

The artwork on each page of this book shows a handshape for the manual alphabet and a corresponding letter of the written alphabet. Other images shown in the art are listed below:

A	Asparagus		N	Nails
B	Bubbles		O	Ornament
C	Cup		P	Paints, Palette
D	Dragonfly		Q	Quilt
E	Eraser		R	Ribbon
F	Fog		S	Stamps
G	Glove		T	Thimbles, Thread
H	Hole		U	Umbrella
I	Icicles		V	Valentine
J	Jam, Jar		W	Web
K	Keys		X	X ray
L	Lace		Y	Yo-yo
M	Mirror		Z	Zipper

The title page shows the handshape for A; the back cover shows the handshape for D; and the front cover shows the handshapes for W, E, H, B, Y, and I.

Acknowledgments

I thank the following people for their help and support:

Everyone at St. Mary's School for the Deaf in Buffalo, New York, especially Sister Virginia Young; Sister Loretta Young; Sister Pauline LeRoy; Tiffany Anderson; Tom (T.J.) Anderson, Jr. and Tom (T.J.) Anderson, Sr.; Jennifer Bump; Norine D. Borkowski; Charlie James Clemente; Jane D'Amico; John Hencker; Bonnie Henderson; Caitlin LaLonde; Samantha Marguccio; Wendy Miller; Sandy Orlando; Lamar James Ray; and Mary Tousley, S.S.J.

Heartfelt thanks to Tony Bannon.

My devotion I send to Aunt Barbara —
who first taught me the manual alphabet — for her love and courage.

Finally, I thank my parents, Ed and Mary Rankin, for their love and example.